Explore .....

Hong Kong: Picture Perfect

Published by Pacific Century Publishers
Reprinted 2004
© 2000 Pacific Century Publishers

Photographs © Cameraman / Keith Macgregor, except pages 5 and 20-21

ISBN # 962-217-668-2

Captions: Hilary Binks

Pacific Century Publishers Limited
Suite 1603-4, Hon Kwok Jordan Centre, 7 Hillwood Road,
Tsimshatsui, Kowloon, Hong Kong
Tel: (852) 2376 2085   Fax: (852) 2376 2137
Email: pacman@pacificcentury.com.hk

Printed in Hong Kong / China

Introduction

Hong Kong begs to be photographed. Its many faces create such a diversity of stunning images that a casual observer might think them to be contrived. But this is not so.

It is true that at first sight the city is one of towering sky scrapers, busy traffic and busier people. Then look again and notice that modern towerblocks are built using ancient bamboo scaffolding, one hundred year-old trams bundle between Mercedes and BMWs' and people still shop for bulk rice and Chinese lanterns. Move out from the city and discover an even greater diversity of style, with rural settings and lifestyles still dictated by the seasons.

No! Hong Kong is not contrived, simply the home of a once migrant population whose strength was their past, their vision the future, and whose achievements are embodied in a great city state.

This book, through its balance of images, sets out to capture the essence of the city and leave the reader with the knowledge that they have truly seen Hong Kong as it moves into the 21st century.

Historic Waterfront

Left: **Hong Kong Island** *Even at night, Hong Kong's Central Business District, seen here looking east towards Wanchai and Causeway Bay, continues to exude energy in a blaze of neon light.*

Above: **Hong Kong Convention & Exhibition Centre** *Jutting into the harbour like a soaring bird, the Hong Kong Convention & Exhibition Centre was the venue for the handover ceremony marking the return of Hong Kong to China in 1997.*

City of Light

Left: **Causeway Bay** *Visitors and locals alike flock to Causeway Bay, one of Hong Kong's most vibrant shopping, hotel and entertainment areas.*

Above: **Trams** *Electric trams, which have trundled along the north shore of Hong Kong Island since 1904, provide an ideal vantage point for the dazzling light show.*

Previous page: **Hong Kong Island** *From a barren rock to one of the most famous skylines in the world, in a mere 150 years!*

Unique Images

Left: **Star Ferry** A great way to see the harbour is aboard a distinctive green and white Star Ferry, which has made regular crossings between Hong Kong Island and Kowloon for over 100 years.

Above: **Bauhinia** This golden representation of Hong Kong's official flower, the bauhinia, also featured on the flag of the Special Administrative Region, was erected to commemorate the handover in 1997.

Left: **Hong Kong Island** Dawn light illuminates the skyscrapers of Central District like fairytale castles which are reflected in the calm waters of the harbour.

Above: **Harbour Cruise** Hong Kong's greatest natural asset is its harbour. Here a tourist vessel steams west towards the Shun Tak Centre and Macau Ferry Pier.

A Chinese City

Left: **Ta Chiu Festival** *Lion dancers are welcomed by village elders in ceremonial robes at the Ta Chiu Festival on the island of Tap Mun in the northeast New Territories.*

Above: **Tradition and Modernity** *The traditional Chinese architecture of a rare surviving mansion contrasts with the 78-storey Central Plaza in Wanchai beyond.*

Left: **Wanchai** *Skyscrapers such as the soaring Central Plaza and the circular Hopewell Centre crowd every available square metre of the most expensive real estate in the world.*

Above, left: **Central** *The Bank of China, designed by Chinese-American architect I.M. Pei, consists of a series of dramatic triangular prisms, topped by twin masts.*

Above, right: **Central** *The high-tech Cheung Kong Centre dwarfs the old Bank of China building between the new Bank of China and Hongkong Bank.*

Previous page: **Celebration Fireworks** *Spectacular firework displays light up the harbour at Chinese New Year.*

The Romance of old Hong Kong

Left: **Chinese Junk** *A traditional Chinese junk with graceful bat-wing sails still makes an occasional appearance in Hong Kong waters.*

Above: **Bamboo Scaffolding** *Agile as circus performers, workers as high as 60 storeys up erect traditional bamboo scaffolding, still standard practice in Hong Kong.*

Previous page: **Hong Kong Island** *Seen from the Kowloon Star Ferry Pier, the waterfront of Wanchai and Central by night makes a breathtaking spectacle.*

Body

and Spirit

Left: **Kwum Yum** *The giant statue of Kwun Yum, Goddess of Mercy, raises her hand in blessing as she looks out to sea at Repulse Bay, on the south side of Hong Kong Island.*

Above: **Jumbo Floating Restaurant** *A ferry from Aberdeen is the only way to reach the glittering Jumbo Floating Restaurant, a famous Hong Kong landmark.*

Previous page: **Chinese Opera** *Vivid colour and dramatic theatrical effects characterise traditional Chinese opera, which is popular in Hong Kong with young and old alike.*

Happy Valley

Left: **Trams** *Trundling round Happy Valley racecourse on their route along the north shore of Hong Kong Island, trams can also be eye-catching mobile billboards.*

Above: **Horse-racing** *This is a local obsession and record-breaking sums of money are bet on races at Hong Kong's two race tracks at Happy Valley and Shatin.*

China's Heritage

Left: **Middle Kingdom** *At the foot of the escalator to Ocean Park, Hong Kong's premier leisure complex, is the Middle Kingdom, an authentic theme park depicting 5,000 years of Chinese history.*
Above: **Giant Panda** *Besides entertainment, Ocean Park has a more serious role, in the conservation of endangered species, including dolphins and giant pandas.*
Previous page: **Dragon Boat Festival** *Competition is fierce between rowing teams taking part in the colourful Dragon Boat Festival held every summer all over Hong Kong.*

Harmony with Nature

Left: South Side, Hong Kong Island
In contrast with the high-rise congestion of the north shore, the south side of Hong Kong Island remains green and relatively unspoilt. In the foreground is the much-favoured residential area of Deep Water Bay with its sheltered yacht anchorage at Middle Island. Through the gap is Repulse Bay and beyond the headland, Tai Tam Bay, with the Lema Islands in the distance.

Sea and Sky

Left: **West Lamma Channel**
*Hong Kong's perfect natural
harbour and its shipping remain
the territory's lifeblood. Every
year Hong Kong plays host to an
amazing number and variety of
craft. Here, as the setting sun
casts a silver gleam over the
Lamma Channel with the
mountains of Lantau Island in
the background, container
vessels steam towards the
container port at Kwai Chung,
the busiest in the world.*

Cultural Vibrancy

Left: **Cultural Centre** *The modernistic Cultural Centre, Hong Kong's principal venue for the performing arts, stands on the Kowloon waterfront behind the old Kowloon-Canton Railway clock tower and opposite the famous Peninsula Hotel.*

Above: **Show Time** *Young pupils from the Jean Wong School of Ballet put on a Chinese New Year performance.*

Previous page: **Kowloon Peninsula** *The hills of Kowloon form a spectacular backdrop to the congested Kowloon Peninsula, a mere 12 square kilometres in area.*

Golden Mile

Left and Above: **Nathan Road and Mong Kok** *Kowloon's main thoroughfare is ablaze with colour at night and shops stay open until the early hours. Colourful, crowded Mong Kok, packed with small shops, restaurants, markets and night clubs, is one of the most traditional Chinese areas of Hong Kong.*
Following page: **North Sai Kung** *Country Parks make up 40% of Hong Kong's territory, including such beautiful scenery as Three Fathoms Cove in Sai Kung.*

Fruits of the Land

Left: **Loi Tung** *This rice paddy, part of an organic farm near Loi Tung established to preserve traditional methods of farming, is now a rarity in Hong Kong.*

Above: **Ta Kwu Ling** *High-quality produce harvested in the closed area on the border with Mainland China is destined for the tables of Hong Kong's top hotels.*

Previous page: **Sha Lo Tung Valley** *The traditional Hakka village of Cheung Uk lies in the unspoilt Sha Lo Tung Valley, New Territories.*

Fresh for the Table

Left: **Women's Work** *Hong Kong people like to buy vegetables fresh each day. Hard-working Hakka women, long the pillars of their matriarchal society, harvest vegetables in the New Territories.*

Above: **Seafood Spectacle** *A wide range of fresh fish and seafood is bought live every day, then often steamed in a sauce of oil, fresh ginger and green onions.*

Previous page: **Hebe Haven** *Chinese root vegetables are dried in the sun before being pickled at a farm in Hebe Haven, Sai Kung, New Territories.*

Lantau Link

Left: **Tsing Ma Bridge** *A key element in the 34-kilometre road and rail network leading to Hong Kong's International Airport at Chek Lap Kok, the Tsing Ma Bridge is the world's longest combined road and rail suspension bridge.*

Above: **Po Lin Monastery** *This statue of a Laughing Buddha is housed in the Po Lin Monastery, Lantau.*

Previous page: **Fishing Junks** *Fishing is still an important activity in Hong Kong and many fisherfolk live aboard their junks.*

Landscape **Man-made**

Left: **Hong Kong Golf Club, Fanling** *Founded in 1889, the Hong Kong Golf Club has three 18-hole courses at Fanling in the New Territories and a nine-hole course at Deep Water Bay, on Hong Kong Island.*
Above: **Airport Link** *An aircraft makes its approach to Chek Lap Kok over Kap Shui Mun bridge, while in the background the Ting Kau Bridge is the start of an express route to the northwest New Territories.*

Architecture as Art

Left: **Chek Lap Kok** *A feeling of light and spaciousness characterises Hong Kong's new airport, built on reclaimed land around a small island in the largest infrastructure project ever undertaken globally.*

Above: **Passenger Terminal** *Designed by Lord Norman Foster, the terminal building is the largest covered structure in the world. It covers 490,000 square metres and can handle 35 million passengers and three million tonnes of cargo a year.*

Spiritual Serenity

*Left: **Kwum Yum Temple, Lantau** One of the most beautiful of the many temples dedicated to Kwum Yum, the Buddhist Goddess of Mercy, worshipped by Taoists and Buddhists alike.*

*Above: **Giant Buddha, Lantau** The world's largest seated outdoor bronze Buddha sits on a lotus throne and a three-tier altar, 268 steps above the Wei To Temple, which acts as an entrance gate to the Po Lin Monastery.*

Farewell .....